Ancient Games © Flying Eye Books 2020.

First edition published in 2020 by Flying Eye Books,
an imprint of Nobrow Ltd. 27 Westgate Street, London E8 3RL.

Illustrations © Avalon Nuovo 2020.

Iris Volant is the pen name of the Flying Eye Books in-house writers.
Text contributions from Moira Butterfield.

Consultant: Kirsty Harding

Every attempt has been made to ensure any statements written as fact have
been checked to the best of our abilities. However, we are still human, thankfully,
and occasionally little mistakes may crop up. Should you spot any errors, please
email info@nobrow.net.

10 9 8 7 6 5 4 3 2 1

Published in the US by Nobrow (US) Inc.
Printed in Poland on FSC® certified paper.

ISBN: 978-1-912497-76-8
www.flyingeyebooks.com

Iris Volant & Avalon Nuovo

ANCIENT GAMES

A HISTORY OF SPORTS AND GAMING

FLYING EYE BOOKS

London | New York

CONTENTS

INTRODUCTION

Even through wars and hardships, humans across the world and throughout history have still had time for a little fun. Since very early times, people have enjoyed competing against each other in sporting events, or watching sports stars showing off their skills. Sports and gaming have formed important parts of rituals and traditions across many cultures, too. From the excitement of chariot races to the ceremonial games of the Aztecs, find out about the sports, and the stars, of years gone by—and cheer alongside ruthless Romans, Chinese emperors, medieval kings, and Viking invaders.

You'll also see that some of these great games are similar to the biggest sporting event in the modern world—the Olympics. Can you imagine watching these iconic games with your ancestors? They wouldn't recognize today's trackside television cameras or hi-tech equipment, but they would surely appreciate the sporting skill and determination on show, because these talents are timeless. Welcome to the world of ancient games.

LET THE GAMES BEGIN

Sports go back thousands of years, to very early human history. Figures that might have been swimming or wrestling appear on cave paintings as far back as 9,000 years ago. We know for sure that wrestling and boxing were sports in the world's first towns and cities—around 5,000 years ago in Sumer (modern day Southern Iraq).

Two wrestlers fight by holding onto each other's belts. This is based on the depiction of wrestlers on a 5,000-year-old Sumerian vase.

WRESTLING HEROES

The oldest known written poem in the world—the Sumerian *Epic of Gilgamesh*—has a wrestling episode in it. The hero Gilgamesh wrestles a wildman from the forest called Enkidu to prove himself strong enough to marry a goddess. According to the poem, these two wrestlers accidentally destroy a doorpost and a wall while they are fighting, but become friends afterward.

BARE KNUCKLES AND BEATS

A clay tablet from Sumeria shows boxers wearing caps and skirts, but no gloves. Musicians are playing drums and cymbals nearby, perhaps to help the fight along and entertain the spectators.

ANCIENT EGYPTIAN GAMES

3100—30 BCE

Ancient Egypt was a powerful kingdom ruled by pharaohs between 5,000 and 2,000 years ago. It stretched along the River Nile in North Africa. We know that the ancient Egyptians played lots of different sports and games because they left carvings, wall paintings, sports equipment, and even board games behind in their tombs. They hoped to take everything from their tombs with them to a new life after death.

In this version of tug-of-war, the front members of the two teams hold onto each other.

WINNING STRENGTH

Staying fit was very important to the Egyptians, in case people were ever called upon to fight in wars. They practiced war skills such as archery and spear-throwing, and played strength games such as boxing, wrestling, and weightlifting (using heavy sacks of grain).

Ancient Egyptian sports often look similar to modern events, but this high jumper is jumping over people, not a pole!

FIT TO RULE

Heb-Sed, also called Sed Festival, was a feast celebrated by the ancient Egyptians. It took place when a pharaoh had ruled for thirty years, then was repeated every three years thereafter. During the celebrations, the pharaoh proved their strength by running around a courtyard racetrack four times.

WINNING IN THE WATER

The River Nile was vital to the ancient Egyptians. It gave them water, rich riverside soil to grow their crops, fish to eat, and a good way to travel through their kingdom. Children learned to swim in the river, and it was used by rowboats. It's thought that the Egyptians also took part in rowing contests and swimming races on the Nile.

WATER-JOUSTING

Ancient Egyptian rowboats had a helmsman standing at one end holding a rudder and shouting instructions to the rowers. Some tomb carvings show teams of men jousting in the water, using poles to try to push each other over. It's not certain whether this was purely for entertainment or was something more violent. For example, these rowers could have been fishermen fighting for fishing territory. Either way, spectators might have watched this exciting water-jousting from their own boats or from the shore.

SWIMMING SKILLS

Swimming races most likely took place in the Nile or the private open-air pools of noblemen. Crocodiles and hippos lived in the Nile, so swimmers would have had to be careful. Despite this, it's likely that most people learned to swim in the river. Some even believed that if someone drowned, it was a good death, because they thought the god of the river would give that person special treatment in the afterlife.

MESOAMERICAN GAMES

Circa 2000 BCE—1500s CE

Mesoamerica is the name given to an area stretching across parts of Mexico, Central America, and South America. It was inhabited by ancient civilizations such as the Maya, Aztecs, and Incas before the arrival of the Europeans around 500 years ago. Games and sports were a big part of these cultures, especially ball contests and board games. Each civilization developed in different places and at different times, but they shared a lot of similarities in the way they played games and sports.

SPORTS FOR GODS

In Maya, Aztec, and Inca cultures, it's likely that most sports and games had religious significance, as well as being fun and exciting. However, the arrival of Europeans in Central and South America changed everything for the cultures they conquered. These Europeans, mainly from Spain, disagreed with many of these religious practices. They had local sports such as ball games banned because of their connections to pagan beliefs.

CLIMB TO THE TOP

The Aztecs had an annual pole-climbing contest for young men during one of their festivals. These young men had to race each other up a 50-foot-high pole made from a tree trunk, using ropes. They grabbed prizes such as warrior's shields, flowers, banners, or the model of an Aztec god made of bread from the top. It's thought whoever reached the bread first would break it into small pieces and throw these toward the spectators below. Everyone attempted to eat a piece of the bread, as a way to give thanks to the gods.

THE GOD OF BOARD GAMES

The Aztecs and Maya are known to have played a board game called "patolli," where players moved a set of pebbles from one end of a board to another using dice. The game was so popular that the Aztecs even had a god for patolli, called Macuilxochitl or Xochipilli. His name means "Prince of Flowers," but he's also known as the "god of good times"— overseeing beauty, art, dance, flowers, and song.

The Aztecs liked to gamble on the outcome of patolli. It's thought they gambled items such as jade beads, valuable bird feathers, or copper bells. Sometimes the stakes were much higher, and they would lose all they had or even gamble themselves into slavery.

READY TO PLAY

Some people carried around mats marked with the cross-shaped game grid wherever they went, to lay down and play patolli in the street. Crowds would gather around the players, and often alcohol was consumed alongside the fun. However, this behavior was disliked by many people, who claimed that the

AN AZTEC BALL COURT

Circa 1400 BCE

Ball games were played across Mesoamerica by most major civilizations including the Maya and Aztecs up to 3,500 years ago. These games normally took place in impressive stone courtyards and were watched by big crowds, most probably at festival times. Over 1,500 ball courts have been found across Central and South America. Many variations of the games existed, including the Maya pok-ta-pok/pok-a-tok and the Aztec ullamaliztli—originating from the words ōlli meaning "rubber" and ōllama meaning "to play ball."

Two teams faced each other on a ball court. They tried to keep a heavy rubber ball off the ground and get it through a stone hoop or across a line without using their hands or feet. They had to move fast and be agile—especially as the result could potentially lead to death.

Human sacrifice was part of religion at this time and many historians think it took place at some ball games. Carvings near some Maya ball courts show players being beheaded, and displays of skulls have been found near some Aztec ball courts. It's hard to know if these sacrifices definitely happened, but it's likely that if they did, the losing players were the people killed.

Ball games were one of the many activities banned by the Europeans who conquered Mesoamerica. Despite this, a version of the ball game still exists today, known as "ulama." Ulama is only played by small groups of people in Mexico, but these players are fighting to teach more and more people about the game, to stop it from disappearing completely.

ANCIENT GREEK GAMES

1100 BCE—600 CE

Ancient Greek civilization was made up of a group of small cities surrounded by countryside called city-states or "poleis." These city-states flourished around the Mediterranean Sea thousands of years ago and were at their most important during "Classical Greece" (500—336 BCE). This is when Greek people wrote great plays, produced stunning sculptures, made incredible scientific breakthroughs, and built grand temples. The ancient Greeks were also known for another long-lasting achievement: organizing the biggest sporting event in the world, the first ever Olympic Games.

DON'T FIGHT, COMPETE

The first Olympic Games that we know of were held in 776 BCE and were a way for city-states to compete without fighting. Instead of going to war, they could send their best male athletes to compete against each other at Olympia, where the games took place. The first recorded Olympic winner was a cook called Koroibos, from the city of Elis. He won a running race called the "stadion," named after the building where it took place.

ATHLETIC ART

Some ancient Greek art took the form of decorated vases and statues. We know from these, and from writings from this period, that the athletes ran naked. At the time, athletic male human bodies were celebrated as the height of beauty.

WINNING FOR ZEUS

The ancient Greeks thought that winning at sport honored the gods they worshipped. Olympia was the site of a temple to Zeus, king of the gods. In the temple there was a giant statue of him sitting on a throne.

The stadion race was about 600 feet long. This is where the word "stadium" comes from.

The ancient Olympic Games initially lasted for just one day, but gradually they grew to five days, with more and more events added. The games were held every four years for over 1,000 years, with big crowds that could reach up to 40,000 spectators. Unfortunately, they finally came to an end in 393 CE, when a Christian Roman emperor called Theodosius banned them because they celebrated pagan gods.

THEN AND NOW

Some of the ancient Olympic events were similar to today's Olympics, such as discus-throwing, the high jump, and javelin-throwing, but others were very different. For instance, in boxing, contestants wrapped leather bandages studded with pieces of sharp metal around their hands and fighters were allowed to break their opponents' fingers.

A WOMAN WINS

Women were not allowed to take part in the Olympic Games and married women were not permitted to watch them either. It's even thought that, if caught, these women could be thrown off a cliff as punishment. Despite this, women had their own separate event called the "Heraean Games" in honor of the goddess Hera. Here, unmarried women would compete against each other in various running sports.

FIRST PLACE

In the ancient Olympic Games there were no gold, silver, or bronze medals. Winners were crowned with a wreath made using olive branches, which were cut from a sacred wild olive tree growing near the temple of Zeus. They also received rewards and honors back in their home city.

CHEAT!

If players were caught cheating they were disqualified, whipped, and fined. The fine money was used to set up bronze statues of Zeus with the cheater's names marked on them. These statues were called the "Zanes of Olympia" and were positioned along the walkway to the stadion, as a warning to all competitors.

MILO OF CROTON

500s BCE

Milo of Croton was one of the biggest sporting superstars of the ancient Olympics. He won the youth wrestling competition in 540 BCE and then won the men's wrestling competition five times. It seemed he was an unbeatable power, until he finally lost to a much younger Olympic wrestler in 512 BCE.

Milo came from Croton, a city in what we now call southern Italy. He was so famous he became a superhero in people's eyes—more like a god than a man. In fact, over time his life story has probably been mixed up with legends of the Greek gods.

It was said he could carry a bull on his shoulders and burst a band around his head by inflating the huge veins on his temples. He's even said to have saved his friends' lives by holding up a roof when a building collapsed. Not only was he strong, but he was also a great fighter and led his city to victory against a neighboring enemy city, wearing a lion's skin and his Olympic wreaths. Sadly, this strength and power didn't keep him from an unfortunate end. Legend has it that he died trying to tear a tree apart to show his strength, but got his hand trapped and was then eaten by wild beasts.

Milo's life legends might not be all true, but the stories about him have inspired painters and sculptors for centuries, making him one of the greatest sporting champions in history.

ANCIENT ROMAN GAMES

753 BCE—478 CE

Ancient Rome was a powerful empire that lasted for over 1,000 years. At its height, it stretched from what is now northern England to northern Africa, across the southern half of Europe and far to the east of modern Turkey. Ancient Roman stadiums called "amphitheaters" were the venues for some Roman games, including fights between gladiators. These contests were brutal and though they didn't always end in death, it's thought that approximately a quarter of them did.

Retiarius

No helmet

Trident

Skills needed:
speed, agility,
and cunning

Short dagger

NET VS. ARMOR

These two different types of gladiator are training against each other in a gladiator school.

SLAVE FIGHTERS

Most gladiators were slaves or criminals who had no choice whether to fight or not. They lived in gladiator schools, where they were trained to be one of several different gladiator types. Each type had different weapons, armor, and fighting methods.

Net

Sword

Secutor

Helmet with tiny eye holes

Armor

Shield

Skills needed: strength and stamina

THUNDERING CHARIOTS

Fast and dangerous chariot races were held in the Circus Maximus, a huge sports arena in ancient Rome. It could hold hundreds of thousands of people, all cheering on their favorite chariot drivers. The races were part of public games held in honor of the Roman gods, and they were free to everyone.

WRAPPED IN REINS

Chariots were drawn by four or more horses. The driver wrapped the reins around his waist, which meant that if there was a crash he risked being tangled up in the wreckage and killed. For this reason, he had a dagger to quickly cut the reins if he needed to escape.

AND THEY'RE OFF!

The chariots exploded from starting gates and had to complete seven laps around the "spina"—a long island down the middle of the track. The drivers could try to make their opponents crash or even pull them out of their chariots. Most crashes happened on the curved corners of the track.

TEAM COLORS

The drivers worked for four famous racing teams in Rome—the Whites, the Greens, the Blues, and the Reds. We know from graffiti written on Roman walls that ancient Romans loved their own team and strongly opposed other teams, just as sports fans do today.

THE COLOSSEUM

Opened 80 CE

The word "amphitheater" means "theater on both sides." They were designed in a round shape so that spectators could see all the action of the gladiator fights. Other events also took place in these amphitheaters, such as wild animal hunts and even naval battles involving water and real ships.

The biggest and grandest amphitheater of all was the Flavian Amphitheater in Rome. Now more commonly known as the "Colosseum," it still stands today, having survived for nearly 2,000 years. It once held a crowd of up to 50,000 screaming, excited Romans hoping to catch a glimpse of some bloodthirsty contests.

Events at the Colosseum were often free because they were paid for by the emperor. Seating had strict rules, meaning only wealthy people had good seats. In some periods, women and slaves were banned completely. The emperor had his own private seating box at the front, with the best view of the action. Here, he could watch every detail and decide if a losing gladiator was killed or spared.

Below the main ring were numerous underground rooms and passages, some of which held wild animals in cages. These cages could be lifted up to release creatures such as elephants, crocodiles, bears, and lions, who were forced to fight gladiators or prisoners also in the ring. It's reported that at the Colosseum's opening games, more than 9,000 animals were killed.

EAST ASIAN GAMES

Circa 400 BCE to present day

China, Japan, North Korea, and South Korea are just a few East Asian countries that have a long history of gaming. The earliest sports from these countries were most likely archery, swordsmanship, and wrestling, practiced by soldiers to keep them fit and ready for battle. China has the longest sporting history and it's even argued they invented some of the most popular sports of today, such as soccer and golf.

FIRST SOCCER

The Chinese have played a kickball game called "cuju" for over 2,000 years. Recognized as one of the earliest forms of soccer, the game took place on a field with one goal and no goalie. The aim was to keep a filled leather ball off the ground, while trying to score. Cuju was a popular sport of the time, played by both men and women. Another form of ancient soccer called "kamari" also originated from East Asia. This Japanese game involves players standing in a circle passing the ball, trying not to let it touch the ground.

KOREAN TUHO

On the Korean Peninsula you can still see lots of traditional sporting games that have been played for centuries. One example is called "Tuho," sometimes known as "pitch-pot." It was popular with nobles 1,000 years ago, and now you can watch it on the internet. Tuho players throw arrow-shaped sticks into a large, sometimes ornate, pot.

CHINESE CARDS

It's thought that playing cards originated from China around 1000 CE or earlier, spreading to Persia, India, Egypt, and then eventually Europe. The earliest written reference to what we believe was a card game comes from a ninth-century Tang Dynasty text. It describes Princess Tongchang and her husband's family playing "yezi ge," meaning "the game of leaves."

It's likely that the first playing cards were wood-block printed paper tiles with patterns and symbols, similar to money bills.

SECRETS OF SUMO

The martial art of sumo wrestling began around 2,000 years ago in Japan and is still popular today. Two wrestlers compete to either propel their opponent out of a ring or force them to touch the ground with any part of their body other than the soles of their feet. Other East Asian countries also have their own martial arts that are similar to sumo, including "ssireum" in South Korea and "boke" in Mongolia.

RELIGION

Sumo first began as a religious ritual that was thought to help the rice crops grow in spring. It still has links with the Japanese religion of Shinto. The wrestlers throw salt into the ring to purify it before they fight, and they clap their hands to summon the gods.

KEEPING UP TRADITION

Sumo is more than just a sport, it is also a glimpse into ancient Japanese clothing and traditions. Sumo wrestlers have topknots, which were fashionable in the 1600s, and they wear traditional dress at all times. Even the referees wear traditional dress, with the most experienced and respected referees wearing elaborate silk costumes.

WINNING WARLORDS

Sumo wrestlers once performed at the court of the Japanese emperor and also for samurai warrior warlords. These warlords trained their own wrestlers and pitted them against those of other warlords. Winning wrestlers would help make their warlord look more powerful and successful.

The wrestling ring where a sumo match takes place is called a "dohyō."

THE LADY OF YUE

Circa 400 BCE

For centuries swordsmanship was a highly valued skill in China and Japan and the best swordsmen took part in contests in front of the emperors. A legendary Chinese woman known as the Lady of Yue has gone down in history as one of the greatest sword experts of all.

The Lady of Yue learned her amazing sword skills to protect herself in the forest where she lived. The ruler of her province, King Goujian, heard of her prowess and sent for her. He set her a test to see just how good she was, and she impressed him by fighting several opponents at once. He appointed her to train his soldiers, and she taught them that agility and speed could be used to defeat stronger opponents. She is said to have invented a new type of flexible sword with very sharp edges.

Nobody knows the real name of the Lady of Yue, or if she even existed, but when King Goujian's tomb was excavated in 1965 a perfectly preserved sword was found, its edges still sharp.

MEDIEVAL EUROPEAN GAMES

Circa 400—1400 CE

The Medieval era (middle ages) was a period in Europe when rulers and their nobles owned all the land, and ordinary people (peasants) worked for them. Nobles took part in sports that needed expensive equipment, such as jousting and an early type of tennis. Peasants had their own simpler sports, such as ball games.

JOUSTING KNIGHTS

When not fighting in wars, knights competed in tournaments to practice their skills and as a form of entertainment. Jousting was a popular sport at these events. Knights would ride against one another with wooden lances, hoping to dismount their opponents. The winners would be treated with respect and admiration, winning money or land if they were really successful.

FIELD SOCCER

Medieval football (soccer) was a free-for-all game played by lots of people at once. Whole villages sometimes took each other on, running around the countryside all day, trying to get the ball. Soccer was regularly banned for being too dangerous and leading to fights!

SPORT OF KINGS

Modern tennis began in medieval Europe as "Royal Tennis," using a ball made of cork and long oval-shaped bats. It's still played today, but it's now called "Real Tennis." It was popular with medieval French and English kings, who built indoor courts in their palaces.

ARROWS AND ARCHERY

Medieval lords could call on their peasants to fight for them at any time, so regular weapons practice was very important. Ordinary men needed to know how to use a bow and arrow or the powerful longbow, and they had to practice by firing at targets. Eventually, archery developed into today's popular Olympic sport.

The target could be anything from a wreath of leaves to a straw mat or ring.

PRACTICE MAKES PERFECT

Laws in mid-1200s England obliged every man between the ages of 15 and 60 to own and know how to use a bow and arrow. Weekly practice took place at "the butts"—earth mounds set up in an open space where targets could be placed.

ARCHERY EQUIPMENT

A longbow was about 6 feet long. The best ones were made of yew wood.

A skilled longbowman could fire 10 to 12 arrows a minute.

Arrows were made of wood with a flat iron head, able to pierce chain mail.

Medieval archers sometimes wore a leather guard called a "bracer" on their bow arm. Modern archers sometimes wear a bracer, too.

Some medieval arrows had feathers on one end, known as the "fletching." This helped the arrow fly in a straight line.

Archers carried their arrows in a "quiver," most likely attached to their belts. These were most commonly made from leather, wood, or fur.

A longbow could reach a target 750 feet away—about the length of two soccer fields!

WILLIAM MARSHAL

Circa 1146—1219

Medieval jousting tournaments were training grounds for young knights, who could win money, armor, and horses in the contests. English knight William Marshal is known as one of the greatest jousters of all time. He must have had word-class horse-riding skills.

William was the son of a minor nobleman. As a younger son, he didn't inherit his father's money or castles, so he had to make his own way in life. As a boy he was nearly killed when his father's castle was besieged and he was caught and held hostage. The hostage takers threatened to hang him or fire him from a catapult!

Young William managed to survive this ordeal, then trained as a knight and became a jousting star. In his time, tournaments were not fought between two knights in an arena. Instead, lots of knights took part, riding around all day across several miles of countryside, trying to unseat each other. An unseated knight had to agree to pay his opponent a ransom before he could get back on his horse. This type of jousting was highly dangerous, not just for the knights but for anyone standing nearby. It's for this reason that the rules were changed, and the one-to-one jousting we might see in modern movies came into fashion.

Later, William became a successful warrior in battle and during his eventful life he was an advisor to four English kings.

VIKING GAMES

793—1066 CE

The Vikings are best known as warriors and traders who came from Scandinavia and traveled far and wide in their longboats. Through trading as well as raiding, Viking culture influenced a huge area of Europe and also had an effect on some areas of North America. They loved sports that championed strength and bravery, but also games that valued cleverness and wit.

WINDOW TO THE PAST

Lots of board games have been found in excavated Viking graves, so we know they were popular and well-loved. In fact, we can actually thank some game pieces for teaching us more about Viking history. In 2017, metal detectorists found hundreds of lead gaming pieces in Lincolnshire, England. This helped to establish the size and location of invading Viking army camps in Britain, some of which may have been bigger than many towns and cities of the time.

GAME OF THE GODS

We know a lot about Viking board games and sports from sagas, which are exciting storylike poems about Viking heroes and gods. In a saga called *Völuspá*, the Viking gods themselves played board games in a meadow, using golden playing pieces.

CLEVER THINKING

Viking game pieces were made from amber, bronze, wood, and even whale and walrus teeth. In one of the games, called "hnefatafl," a king and his small band of warriors must escape an ambushing army and get to safety. The game has been compared to chess, and the players had to think cleverly to outwit their opponent.

The king was often the most impressive piece in hnefatafl. It would sit in the middle of the board surrounded by other pieces.

WELCOME TO THE LEIKMÓT

We know from their sagas that Vikings sometimes gathered for a sports and games meeting called a "leikmót." These meetings were held in the fall and would have been a chance for some fun before winter set in. Men took part in all sorts of physical sports at the leikmóts, as well as enjoying themselves with feasts and celebrations.

The bat and ball game knattleikr was played on ice or grass and could go on for hours.

BAT AND BALL GAMES

We know that the Vikings played a rough-and-tumble bat and ball team game called "knattleikr." Like a cross between baseball and rugby, the game involved hitting a ball with a stick, catching the ball and running with it. Players could tackle each other and they sometimes ended up in fights!

WINNING WARRIOR STRENGTH

Tug-of-war competitions, wrestling, and lifting up or throwing heavy stones were all leikmót events. These were all sports that took immense strength, as this was an important attribute for Viking men. After all, they might have to row longboats long distances, as well as fight their enemies.

FEASTING GAMES

The Vikings would gather in the halls of their chieftains to play all sorts of other activities, too. One game involved throwing a rolled-up bearskin around and someone would try to grab it. Throwing bones and catching them was also popular after a big feast

ANCIENT GAMES TO MODERN OLYMPICS

1896 to present day

Not all ancient games disappeared into history, as shown most clearly by the revival of the Olympic Games. The modern Summer Olympics began in 1896 and many of its events are inspired by the ancient games, with the same ideals of unifying people and inspiring competitive spirit. Baron Pierre de Coubertin is considered the father of the modern games— he fought hard to reinstate them and was the first chairperson of the International Olympics Committee. To keep with tradition, and as a mark of respect, the first modern games were held in Athens, Greece.

The first event in the modern Olympics was
a qualifying round for the 100 meter race.

FATHER OF THE OLYMPICS

Over time, Pierre de Coubertin brought in many features that are now in the modern games. The most iconic are the famous Olympic rings symbol and the Olympic flame. When Pierre died, his heart was buried at the site of the ancient Olympics, Olympia.

The five interlocking Olympic rings were created to represent the five inhabited continents of the world.

The Olympic flame is an ode to the ancient games, where a flame was kept alight throughout the ceremonies. It reflects the myth of Prometheus, who stole fire from the gods and gave it to humanity.

AND THEY'RE OFF!

There were forty-three events in the first modern Olympics. Some we know today and some more unusual ones, such as one-handed weightlifting and a swimming race just for the Greek Navy. There were 245 male competitors from fourteen countries, but women were still not allowed to compete. The ceremonies and rules had not yet been properly worked out, though these gradually developed over future games.

OLYMPIC EVOLUTION

The Summer Olympics are held every four years and have progressed and changed a great deal over time. These changes are most evident in the stricter rules, the advanced technology, and the entry requirements. The games have also expanded to be more inclusive, with the addition of new sports and sporting events.

Even though women were able to compete they were still expected to wear "proper" clothing, which wasn't comfortable or sensible for playing sports.

WOMEN ALLOWED

The first modern Olympics were the only ones without women. At the Paris Olympics in 1900, twenty-two women competed in tennis, sailing, horse riding, golf, and croquet. At the time, running was thought to be dangerous for women's health, so women didn't take part in track events until 1928. In fact, women did not run in an Olympic race over 200 meters until 1960.

MORE FOR ALL

Over time the Summer Olympics have been joined by the Paralympics, Winter Olympics, Youth Olympics, and Special Olympics. The Paralympics are now the second biggest sporting event in the world, with around 4,000 disabled athletes competing in over twenty different sports. New sports are regularly chosen for the Olympics, too. Karate, skateboarding, baseball/softball, sport climbing, and surfing joined the events list for the 2020 Tokyo Summer Games.

Paralympians are able to compete in some sports that do not appear in the Summer Olympics, such as blind football, wheelchair rugby, and sitting volleyball.

MODERN OLYMPIC CHAMPIONS

2008, 2012, 2016

There have been many inspiring Olympic competitors throughout the years. Here are just some stories of those who've touched millions of fans with their achievements. They have the determination and talent of the sports stars who came hundreds, even thousands, of years before them—but thanks to television and the internet, they have been watched by millions more fans!

ELLIE SIMMONDS

British swimmer Ellie Simmonds is one of many awe-inspiring Paralympians. She was born with a condition that restricted her growth, but when she started swimming at five, nothing could stop her. At just thirteen, she won two gold medals in the 2008 Paralympics and smashed world records to win gold again in 2012 and 2016.

SIMONE BILES

US artistic gymnast Simone Biles took the 2016 Rio de Janeiro Olympics by storm when she smashed records and became a four-time gold medal winner at just nineteen. She's also won multiple World Championships and some consider her to be the best of all time in her sport. In her early life she was in foster care, but she overcame the difficulties in her childhood to become one of the greats.

REFUGEE TEAM

Ten athletes* made Olympic history at the 2016 Rio de Janeiro games by competing for the Refugee Team for the first time. They were all refugees who had escaped war and had no home, no flag, and no national anthem. Competing under the Olympic flag, they all showed us what it takes to be great sports people in any age—huge amounts of spirit and determination, no matter the odds.

* Rami Anis (swimming), Yiech Biel (track and field), James Chiengjiek (track and field), Yonas Kinde (track and field), Anjelina Lohalith (track and field), Rose Lokonyen (track and field), Paulo Lokoro (track and field), Yolande Mabika (judo), Yusra Mardini (swimming), Popole Misenga (judo)

The way we all play games and sports is developing fast, thanks to new technology and changing mindsets. Big sports events such as the Olympic Games aren't just becoming more inclusive, but are aiming to become more environmentally friendly, too. However, the reasons humans take part in sports—to win and to have fun—will surely be the same for years to come.

SPORT GETS GREEN

The International Olympic Committee has added something new to its aims. As well as promoting sport, the Olympics must also promote caring for the environment. This means that the games will now recycle as much as possible and use renewable energy at all sites. Tokyo 2020 has taken this initiative in its stride, using recycled metals for medals and recycled clothing for athletic uniforms. These small changes are more important now than ever, as climate change has already begun to affect the Winter Olympics, with less predictable cold weather bringing problems for outdoor winter sports.